ILLUSTRATIONS

OF

ANCIENT BUILDINGS IN KASHMIR

ILLUSTRATIONS
OF
ANCIENT BUILDINGS
IN KASHMIR.

BY
HENRY HARDY COLE

GYAN

Published by

Gyan Publishing House
5, Ansari Road
Daryaganj, New Delhi-110002
Phone: 011-47034999, 9811692060
E-mail: books@gyanbooks.com

Distribution Network
gyanbooks.com
India, USA, Canada, UK, Australia, France

ISBN: 978-93-6280-620-8 (PB)

First Published, 1869

2nd Impression 2023

Printed at: Gyan Press, Delhi.

ILLUSTRATIONS OF ANCIENT BUILDINGS IN KASHMIR

Author: HENRY HARDY COLE

ILLUSTRATIONS

OF

ANCIENT BUILDINGS IN KASHMIR.

PREPARED UNDER THE AUTHORITY OF

THE SECRETARY OF STATE FOR INDIA IN COUNCIL

FROM

PHOTOGRAPHS, PLANS, AND DRAWINGS

TAKEN

BY ORDER OF THE GOVERNMENT OF INDIA.

BY

HENRY HARDY COLE, LIEUTENANT, R.E.

SUPERINTENDENT, ARCHÆOLOGICAL SURVEY OF INDIA, NORTH-WEST PROVINCES.

LONDON:
INDIA MUSEUM,
1869.

Wm. H. ALLEN AND CO., 13, WATERLOO PLACE, S.W.
PUBLISHERS TO THE INDIA OFFICE.

This Work forms the first in the Series of Volumes which it is proposed to publish in connexion with the operations of the Archæological Survey of India.

The Illustrations have been produced from the original negatives in the Photographic Department of the India Museum, by the "Autotype" Process in Carbon, and are therefore permanent.

NOTICE.

THE Photographs and photographed Drawings contained in this series were taken in the latter end of the year 1868. I left Cawnpore on the 1st September, and, accompanied by two native surveyors, Thakoor Dass and Habeeb-oo-lah, travelled through Delhi, Lahore, and Rawul Pindee to Murree, where the Lieutenant-Governor of the Punjab was staying during the hot weather. At Murree our camp was formed for marching into Kashmir, and on September the 29th we commenced the journey to Srinagar. On the 10th October we found ourselves in the valley of Kashmir, and from this day to the 3rd November, the surveyors with myself were occupied in visiting the various buildings here illustrated. The lateness of the season limited our operations much, and many Temples of great interest had to be passed over; it would, however, have been impracticable to lengthen our stay in the valley, as the snow threatened to block up the passes leading to the Plains of India.

Mr. Burke, a photographer of Murree and Peshawur, formed one of our party. The zeal which he displayed in his work, and the successful manner in which he completed it, entitle him to great credit.

HENRY H. COLE,
Lieutenant, R.E.,
Superintendent Archæological Survey of India,
North-western Provinces.

October 1869.

CONTENTS.

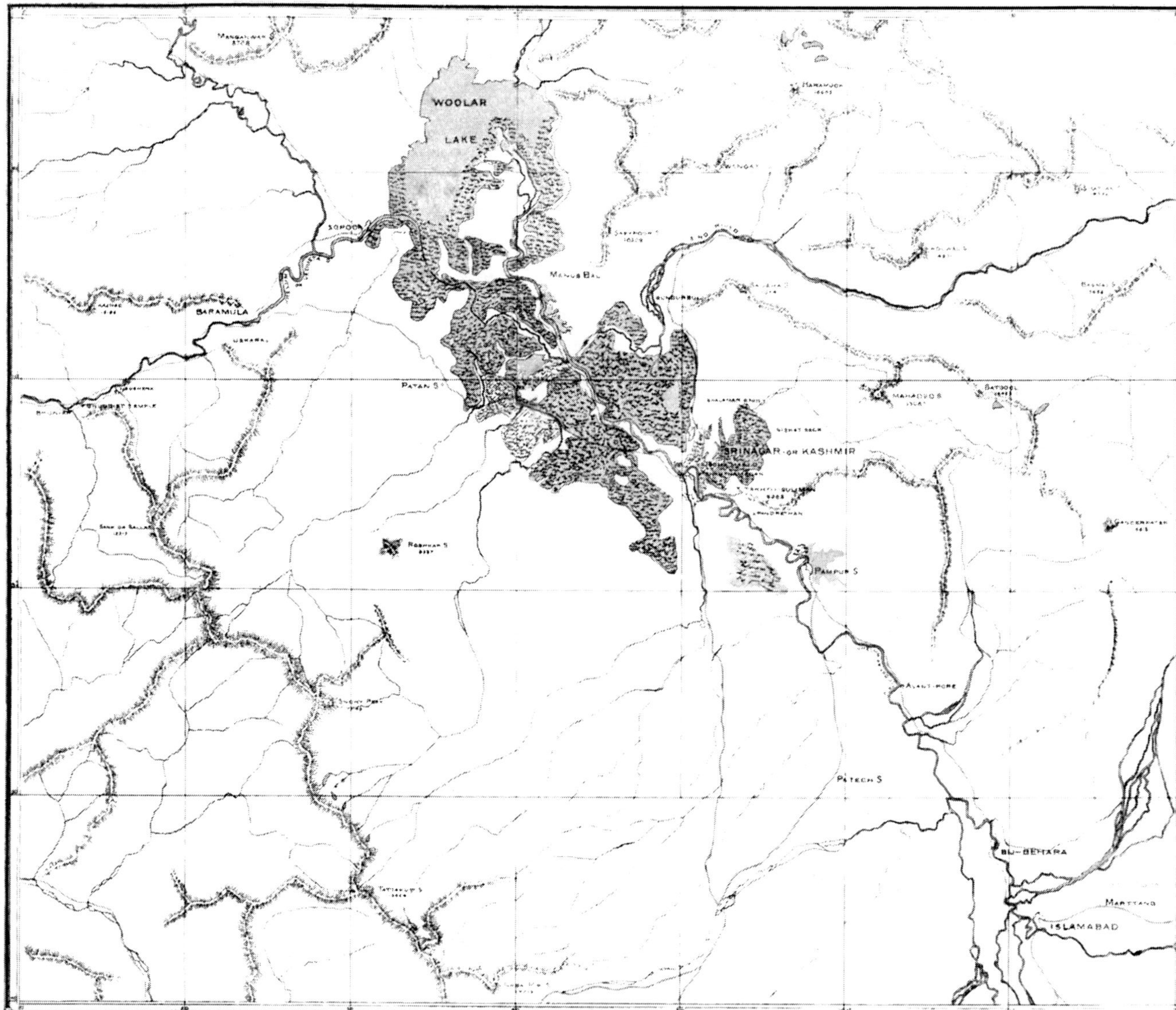

W. GRIGGS, DEL. & LITH.

INDIA MUSEUM, LONDON 1869.

SKELETON MAP OF KASHMIR

SCALE OF MILES

NOTES ON ANCIENT BUILDINGS IN KASHMIR.

TEMPLE ON THE TAKT-I-SULIMAN HILL.

THE Takt-i-Suliman Hill overlooks Srinagar, the Capital of Kashmir; standing one thousand feet above the plain, it commands a noble view of the Valley and its surrounding ridges of snow-topped peaks.

On its crest stands the most ancient building in Kashmir—the Temple of Jyeshteswara,* which, according to tradition, has existed since 220 B.C.; near it, on the right,† is a smaller building, and in front are the ruined remains of a third. The Temple of Jyeshteswara rests on the solid rock, and consists of an octagonal stone basement twenty feet high, on which is supported a square building: on each of the four sides are two projections which terminate in a pediment and a gable, the latter intersecting the main roof half-way up its slope.

The body of the Temple is surrounded by a terrace enclosed by a low wall or parapet,‡ which in following the outline of the basement preserves its octagonal shape.

In later years this feature of an enclosing wall was destined to be elaborated into noble colonnades, like those of Avantipore, Marttand, and Bhaniyar.

---

* See Photographs 1 and 2—'68.

† See Drawing 1—'68.

‡ See Drawing 1—'68, Section; and Details A and B.

The terrace surrounding the Temple is reached by a stone staircase encased between two walls,* and a doorway, exactly opposite, leads to the interior, which is a small and dark chamber, circular in plan. The ceiling is supported by four octagonal columns, which surround a Basin containing a Lingam encircled by a snake. The walls are eight feet in thickness, and are therefore proof of the great antiquity of the building. On the left pillar shown in the sectional elevation and detail of the Temple are two Persian inscriptions,† which have been engraved on two of the adjacent octagonal sides. The first reads 'The architect of this pillar is the supplicant Bihishti . . . . the fifty-fourth year.' The second is confused, but begins 'This pillar,' so that both probably have reference to the time when the temple was repaired, as evidenced by the present character of the roof, which is not the original pyramidal shape, but a clumsy brick covering, surmounted by a melon-like ornament. There are also two mutilated inscriptions on each of the two flank walls encasing the staircase; the character is Persian, and the date A.H. 1069 or A.D. 1659. General Cunningham says of this Temple, 'It is now called Sankaráchára, but the Brahmins in the valley were unanimous in their belief that its original name was Jyeshteswara. Its erection they ascribed to *Jaloka*, the son of Asoka, who reigned about 220 B.C.'

The whole of the building is of stone, which is laid throughout in horizontal courses,‡ no cement appearing to have been employed. This horizontal treatment is peculiar to most Hindú buildings in India, and is adhered to in all the ancient examples of Kashmir. The style of the Temple represented in the accompanying photographs and plan, reproduces itself throughout in all the Hindú Kashmirian buildings. The high-pitched pyramidal roof, the one, two, or more gables or pediments, the enclosing wall, and the character of the base mouldings,§ are features common to

---

* See Drawing 1—'68, Plan and Elevation.

† See Drawing 1 A—'68.

‡ See Drawing 1—'68, Elevation.

§ See Drawing 1—'68, Detail C.

all; but this building more than others of its style shows so close an affinity to the form of the common Hindú Temple of Bengal, that we may suppose both to owe their existence to some common origin, without any great stretch of fancy. In Bengal the pediments and gables are slightly curved, and much more numerous, but in both Kashmir and Bengal the primary form was the square block surmounted by a pyramidal roof. The mode of elaborating the plan remained the same in both countries, and consisted in the addition of one or more projections to each of the original four sides of the square.

KASHMIR.

Temple of JYESHTESWARA, on the TAKT-I-SULIMAN HILL, near SRINAGAR. Probable date 220 B.C.

No. 1. '68.

KASHMIR.

Temple of JYESHTESWARA, on the TAKT-I-SULIMAN HILL, near SRINAGAR. Probable date 220 B.C.

No. 2. '68.

KASHMIR. 1.-'68.

RESTORATION.

TEMPLE OF JYESHTESWARA OR SANKARACHARYA ON THE TAKHT-I-SULIMAN HILL, SRINAGAR.

PROBABLE DATE-B. C. 220.

A

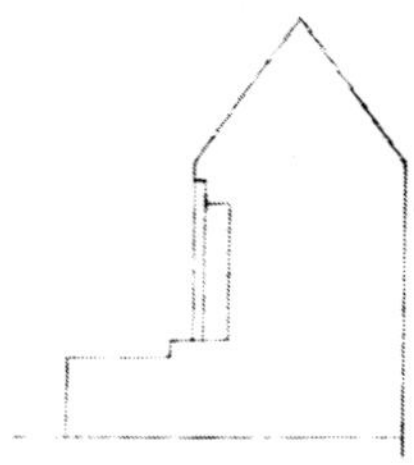

SECTION THROUGH ENCLOSING WALL.

B

ELEVATION OF ENCLOSING WALL.

ELEVATION.

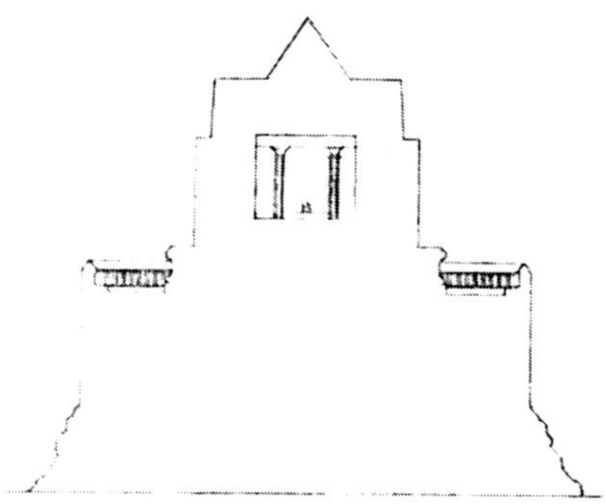

SECTION.

SCALE OF FEET

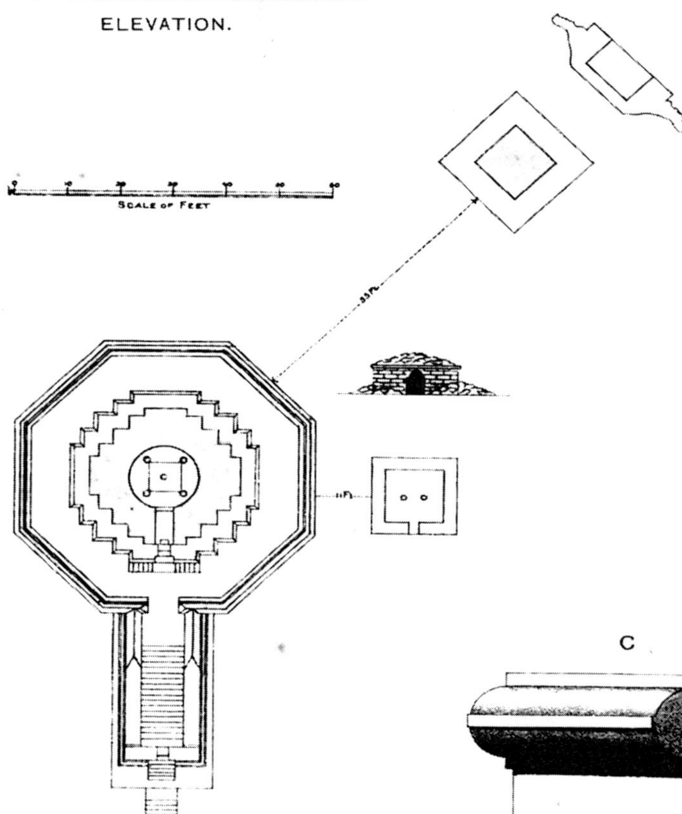

PLAN.

D

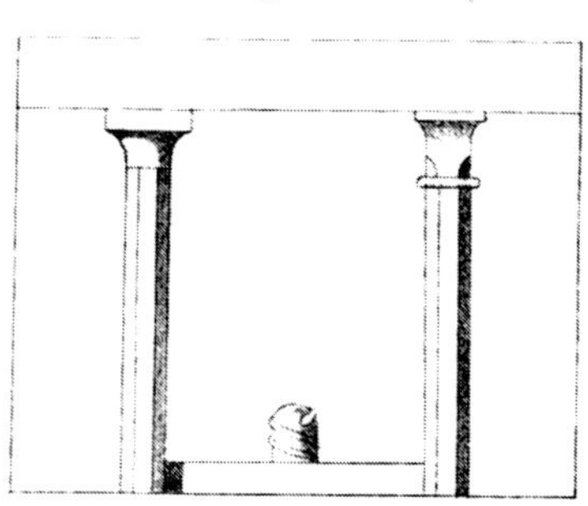

DETAIL OF TEMPLE.

C

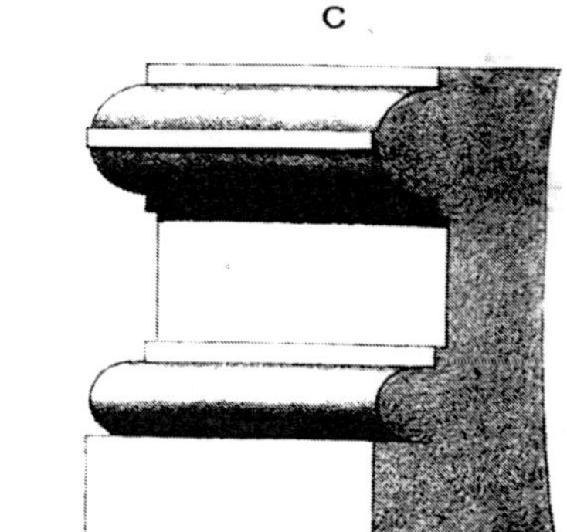

DETAIL OF BASE.

SCALE OF DETAILS-A-B-C

SCALE OF DETAIL D

H. H. Cole Lieut R.E.
Supt. Archl. Survey of India
North Western Provinces.

W. GRIGGS. DEL. & LITH.

INDIA MUSEUM, LONDON 1869.

TWO INSCRIPTIONS ON TWO SIDES OF AN OCTAGONAL PILLAR (ONE OF FOUR) IN THE TEMPLE OF JYESHTESWARA, ON THE TAKHT-I-SULIMAN HILL, NEAR SRINAGAR.

W. GRIGGS. DEL. & LITH.

INDIA MUSEUM, LONDON 1868.

GROUPS OF TEMPLES AT RAJDAINBAL AND NAGBAL, NEAR WANGAT.

THESE two Groups of Temples are situated in the valley of the river Kanknai, about three miles beyond the small village of Wangat, and are reached by a narrow unfrequented path which winds through thick forest above the river.

The two Groups are separated by about 200 yards, and both are very much surrounded and enclosed by trees; the situation is indeed so secluded that a quantity of pine and fir had to be felled with the axe, before either photographs or measurements could be taken.

The way to these Temples from Srinagar is by Ganderbal, and the journey can be accomplished in two marches, one of about ten, and the other of about fifteen miles.

The locality of the Temples nearer to Wangat is known by the name of Rajdainbal.* This Group consists of six buildings, all more or less ruined, and the remains of an enclosing wall, measuring 176 feet long by 130 feet wide, may still be traced, although there is no evidence of the form it took, whether that of a simple enclosure, like that round the Temple on the Takt-i-Suliman Hill, or that of a colonnade, as in the case of the more elaborate and modern Kashmirian Temples. The largest Temple of the Group measures 24 feet square, and has a projection on each of its four sides, measuring 3 feet by 15 feet 6 inches.

---

* See Photographs 8—'68, and 9—'68; and Plan 7—'68.

The main block is surmounted by a rubble pyramidal roof, formerly, no doubt, faced with stone; and the gables which terminated the porch-like projections on all four sides can still be traced. There are two entrances, facing east and west.

The principal Temple of this Group is in a better state of preservation than any of those at Nagbal. The dome and roof are of masonry, and both maintain their original vaulted and pyramidal forms. A large quantity of stones, of huge dimensions, lie heaped in the enclosure; among them some drums of stone columns, which are so weather worn that it is impossible to say whether they were fluted or simple rounded pillars.

The two doorways and side recesses show signs of elaborate carving; but destructive influences have been so actively and successfully at work, that no definite forms can be traced.

I failed, after a careful search in every likely place, to find any trace of an inscription, and am able to support my idea of the date of the buildings in this locality, by no better evidence than the state and style of the architectural details, which in their general simplicity of form and outline should, I imagine, rank in age after the Takt-i-Suliman Temple. After having carefully compared these Temples with others of more authenticated date in the valley, I conclude that the period of their erection would probably coincide with the commencement of the Christian era. In all but the presence of a trefoil-headed arch and more elaborate detail, the Temples are the exact copy of that of Jyeshteswara,* the date of which General Cunningham has assumed, on the evidence of the Raja Tarangini's writings, to be 220 B.C.

A tall fir and other trees have grown on the pyramidal roof of the principal Temple, and it was probably by their expansion that the outer stone facing became displaced.

---

* See Photographs 1—'68 and 2—'68.

At a short distance beyond this Group and on the path leading to the Nagbal Ruins, is a rectangular platform, 100 feet by 67 feet, which appears to have been the basement of some building or temple. A colonnade once existed all round it,—numerous bases of pillars are in their places on one of the longer sides of the rectangle, and several fragments of fluted columns are lying about, their average diameter being 2 feet.

The second Group of Temples, which is situated at Nagbal, just beyond Rajdainbal, numbers seven buildings, the principal one being 25 feet square, with projections on each face. The situation is a very wild one, and much overgrown, and the buildings themselves are in a most ruinous condition. There appears to have been little or no carving on any one of them, but it is difficult to say whether the absence of any such signs may or may not be due to natural decay.

A mass of stone measuring 22 feet by 7 feet, shaped into a tank for water, exists on the south face of the principal Temple, and bears witness, I should say, to the antiquity of the buildings. The whole Group is encircled by the remains of a rectangular wall, of which the foundations can be traced, together with several bases of pillars; and at the north-west corner, is a large tank of stone filled with the coldest and clearest water.

The dome of the chief Temple—such as now remains—is of rubble masonry, but all the other parts of the building are of stone.

As in the case of the Rajdainbal Group, and by the same reasoning, I have assumed the age of these buildings to date from about the commencement of the Christian era, but on account of a greater simplicity, and in the absence of carvings, I should think they might, if anything, be a few years earlier.

The chief peculiarities of these ruins, are the number of Temples contained within the same enclosing wall, and the absence of symmetry in their arrangement. It may, I think, be thus argued: in earlier times, when the enclosing wall was but a mere means of protection, a number of detached

Temples were erected and dedicated to various Deities, whilst the colonnade of later years, was but the symmetrical and systematic arrangement of such buildings in connexion with cells for the officiating Priests, the principal Temple occupying as before, the place of honour in the centre of the enclosed court.

KASHMIR. 6.-'68.

RESTORATION.

GROUP OF TEMPLES AT NAGBUL

NEAR WANGAT.

PROBABLE DATE A.D. 1.

EAST

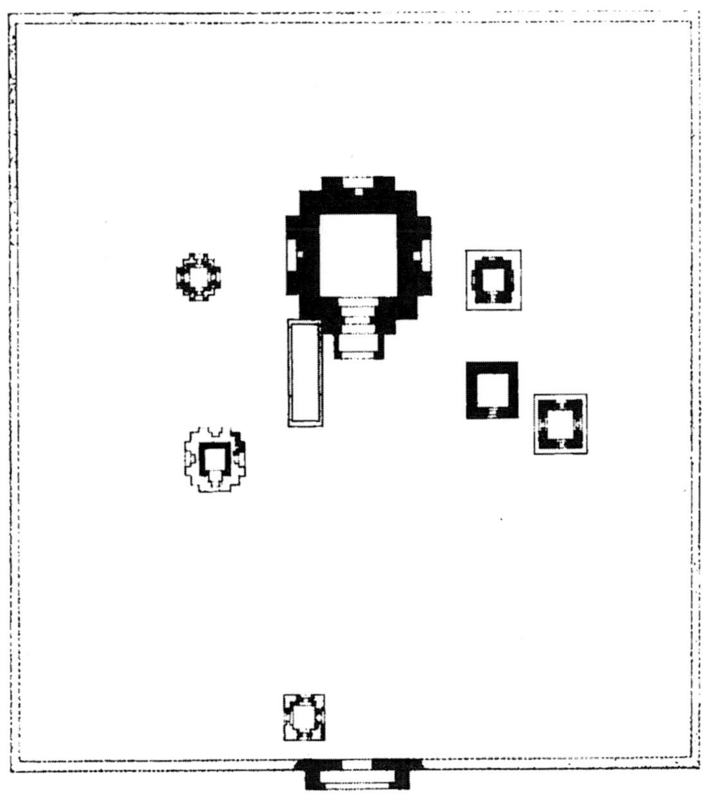

WEST

REFERENCE.

Existing Portions
Restored Portions

GENERAL PLAN.

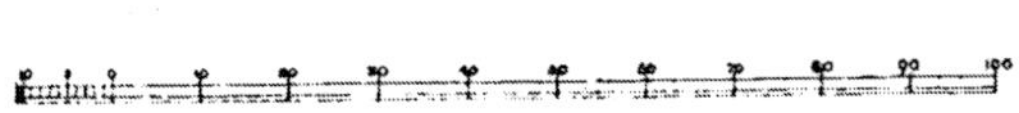

SCALE OF FEET.

H. H. Cole
Lieut R.E.
Supt. Archl. Survey of India
North Western Provinces

W. GRIGGS, DEL. & LITH.

INDIA MUSEUM, LONDON 1869.

KASHMIR.

Second Group of Temples near the Village of Wangut in the Scind Valley. View of largest temple looking South East. Probable date A.D. 1 (?) No. 6. '68

KASHMIR.

Second Group of Temples near the Village of Wangut in the Scind Valley. View of South East face.
Probable date A.D. 1 (?) No. 7. '68

KASHMIR.

First Group of Temples near the Village of Wangut in the Scind Valley. View of principal Temple looking North.

Probable date A.D. 1 (?) No. 8. '68

KASHMIR.

First Group of Temples near the Village of Wangut in the Scind Valley. View of principal Temple looking West.
Probable date A.D. 1 (?) No. 9. '68

KASHMIR.

RESTORATION.

7.–'68.

GROUP OF TEMPLES AT RAJDAINBUL

NEAR WANGAT.

PROBABLE DATE A.D. 1.

SOUTH

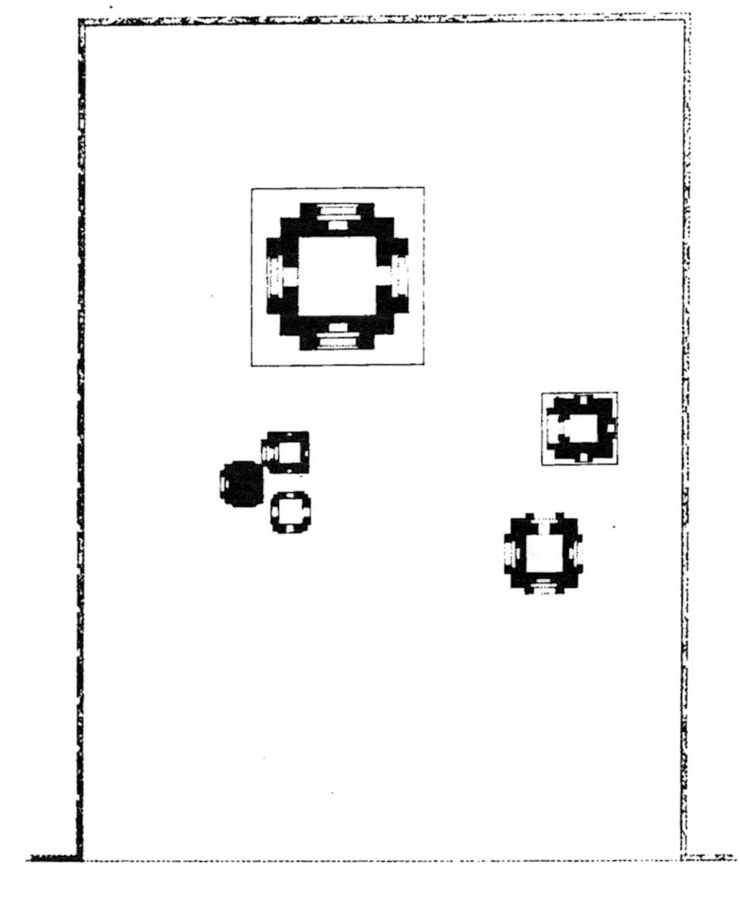

NORTH

GENERAL PLAN.

W. GRIGGS. DEL. & LITH.

SCALE OF FEET

H. H. Cole, Lieut. R.E.

Supt. Archl. Survey of India.

North Western Provinces.

INDIA MUSEUM, LONDON 1869.

ENCLOSURE ROUND ZEIN-UL-AB-UD-DIN'S TOMB, IN SRINAGAR.

THE Tomb of Sikander's Queen is built on the foundations and with the materials of an ancient Hindu Temple; and during the reign of that monarch (who died in 1416 A.D.), a vast desecration and demolition of Hindu buildings took place.

The Queen's Tomb can just be seen in the right-hand corner of photograph 3—'68; to the left of it, and in the same picture, is the Enclosure which once surrounded a Hindu Temple, but which now contains the Tomb of Sikander's Son Zein-ul-ab-ud-din.

Photograph 5—'68 gives an enlarged view of the entrance to this enclosure, and the general plan and details are shown in Plan 8—'68.

The two Gateways in Photographs 4—'68 and 5—'68 have been restored by the Mahomedans, a brick arch having been added in both cases, but in the other details may be traced the progress of the Kashmirian style, and the development of the enclosing wall into a colonnade.

On comparing the details marked A and B in both drawings, 1—'68 and 8—'68, it will be at once seen how the tendency was to increase the elaboration in the wall.

In the Panels of the Gateways, there is proof that buildings had previously existed, in which columns played a part, for it is hardly to be supposed that such a form in detail should precede the original construction. The break in the roof is also remarkable as occurring in conjunction with the simplicity of the enclosing wall, and indicates, I think, that the Gateway is probably more modern than the wall, and may perhaps have been set up by the Mahomedans out of some of the materials of other ruined temples, of which a quantity lies strewn all over Srinagar.

KASHMIR.

Enclosure, (once of a Hindu Temple) of Zein-ul-ab-ud-din's Tomb, in Srinagar.
Probable date A.D. 400 to 500 (?) No. 3. '68.

KASHMIR.

Gateway of Enclosure, (once of a Hindu Temple) of Zein-ul-ab-ud-din's Tomb, in Srinagar.
Probable date A.D. 400 to 500 (?) No. 5. '68.

KASHMIR.

RESTORATION.

8.-'68.

ENCLOSURE
(ONCE OF AN HINDU TEMPLE)
OF ZEIN-UL-AB-UD-DIN'S TOMB,
IN SRINAGAR.

PROBABLE DATE-A.D. 400-500 ?.

A

SECTION THROUGH ENCLOSING WALL.

B

ELEVATION OF ENCLOSING WALL.

ELEVATION.

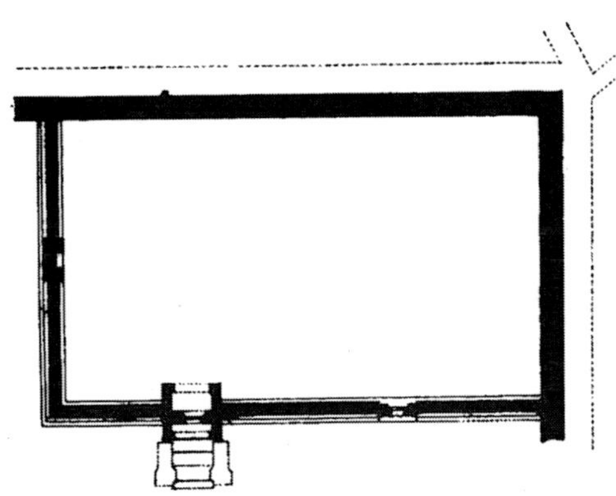

PLAN.

C

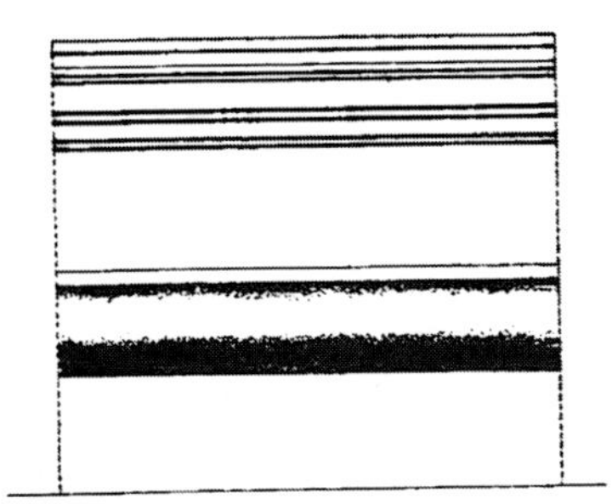

DETAIL OF BASE.
ELEVATION.

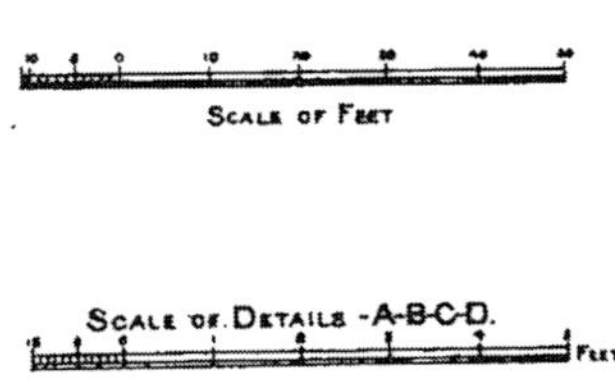

D

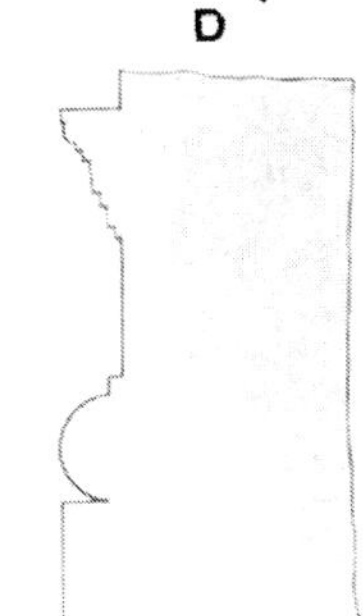

DETAIL OF BASE.
SECTION.

H. H. Cole Lieut. R.E.
Supt. Archl. Survey of India
North Western Provinces

W. GRIGGS. DEL. & LITH.

INDIA MUSEUM, LONDON 1869.

KASHMIR.

Gateway leading to Enclosure, (once of a Hindu Temple) of Zein-ul-ab-ud-din's Tomb, in Srinagar.
Probable date A.D. 400 to 500 (?) No. 4. '68.

ANCIENT TEMPLE BETWEEN URI AND NAOSHERA.

THIS Temple is marked on the Skeleton Map as a " Buddhist Temple," but Baron Hugel is the only authority who alludes to it as being Buddhist. General Cunningham supposes it to have been a Hindu Temple, which formerly contained an image of Durgá. As may be seen from the Photograph,* the overgrowth of trees and weeds is great, and the building is in a state of ruin. The presence of colonnades would indicate that the building occurred about the fifth century.

---

* Photograph No. 39—'68.

KASHMIR.

Temple on the road between Uri and Naoshera. Probable date A.D. 400 (?)

No. 39. '68.

TEMPLE OF MARTTAND, OR THE SUN.

THE most impressive and the grandest ruins in Kashmir, are at Marttand,* which is about three miles east of Islamabad.

This Temple has been the subject of much controversy in respect of its age and dedication, but I believe with General Cunningham that the dedication was to the Sun, Matan being but a corruption of the Sanskrit Marttand, or "the Sun." Mention is made in the following verse of the Raja Tarangini, translated by M. Troyer, "Il construisit aussi dans le village "Sinharotsika un sanctuaire au Soleil, lequel sous le nom de Ranapuraswámi, "acquit une renommée répandue partout." General Cunningham explains that the name of the Temple is Ranapuraswami, or as called in the following verse "Ranesa," both terms meaning "Lord of Rana," or Ranâditya, and implying the devotion of the latter to Siva. M. Troyer, however, expressly declares in his translation, that the Temple was dedicated to the Sun; General Cunningham believes that two different edifices were indicated in the above verse: first, the Temple of Ranapuraswami, dedicated to Siva; and, second, the Temple of Marttand, mentioned by the Raja Tarangini as that surrounded by the colonnade. The Rajah Tarangini goes on to say that, "Amrita Prabhá, one of the King's (Ranâditya's) wives, erected an "'Amriteswara' close to the south side of Ranésa." So that three

* See Photographs, 10, 11, 12, 13, 14, 15, 16, 17, 19—'68.

Temples are mentioned, which correspond with those now known by the name of Marttand:

*1. The principal Temple, dedicated to Marttand, or the Sun.

2. Small Temple to the north, named Ranapuraswami, and dedicated to Siva.

3. The Temple of Amriteswara, due south.

Ranaditya, according to all accounts, was a very powerful Prince, and native writers have accredited him with the miraculous reign of 300 years. This has naturally given rise to much speculation as to the period of his reign, but General Cunningham places it as between A.D. 480 and 555. The date therefore of the two smaller Temples of Ranesa† and Amriteswara‡ may be assumed as about A.D. 500.

The large Temple, dedicated to the Sun, was probably of earlier date, and may possibly have been erected by Arya Raja (A.D. 360 to 383), who, with exception of the Buddhist Prince Meghavahana (A.D. 383 to 400), was one of the only rich predecessors of Ranâditya, and a worshipper of the Emblems of Saīva.

According to the testimony of the Raja Tarangini, the colonnade§ was built by Lalitaditya, who reigned in Kashmir from A.D. 693 to 729; and the character of the fluted columns, would lead to the supposition that the architects of Kashmir had been influenced by those of the Græco Bactrians. The main building contains three distinct chambers; the outermost one is called the "Arddha-mandapa," or "half temple;" the middle one, "Antarala," or "mid temple;" and the inner one called "Garbha-griha," or the "womb of the edifice." The central chamber is richly ornamented, as may be seen

---

* See Plan 5—'68.

† See Plan 5—'68, D. ‡ See Plan 5—'68, E.

§ See Photograph 19—'68; and Plan 5—'68.

from the panels or niches in the detail photographs, 14, 15, 16, 17, 18—'68. The inner chamber is perfectly plain, but the outer one is much decorated. It is now difficult to realize the extreme beauty of the external decoration, as the stone carvings have been terribly mutilated by the Mahomedans; enough, however, is existing to prove that the Temple had been covered with ornamental carvings of a high class.

KASHMIR.

5.-'68.

RESTORATION.

COLONNADE AND TEMPLE OF MARTTAND
OR THE SUN.

DATE OF TEMPLE-A.D. 490-555.
DATE OF COLONNADE-A.D. 693-729.

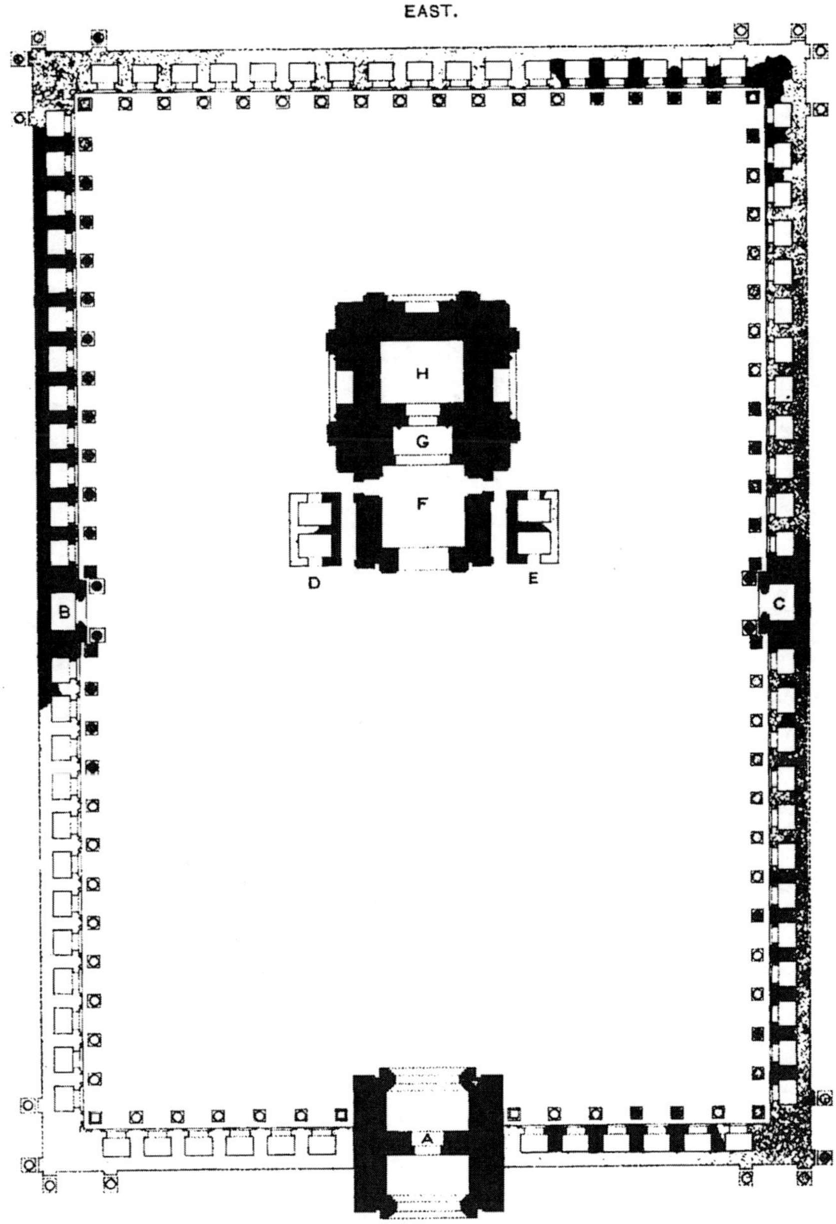

REFERENCE

EXISTING ...... } PORTIONS
RESTORED ......

GENERAL PLAN.

SCALE OF FEET

H. H. Cole
Lieut. R.E.
Supt. Arch. Survey of India
North Western Provinces

W. GRIGGS. DEL. & LITH.

INDIA MUSEUM, LONDON 1868.

KASHMIR.

General View of Temple and Enclosure of MARTTAND OR THE SUN, near Bhawan. Probable date of Temple A.D. 490-555. Probable date of Colonnade A.D. 693-729. No. 10. '68

KASHMIR.

Temple of Marttand or the Sun. View looking East. Probable date A.D. 490-555.

No. 11. '68

KASHMIR.

KASHMIR.

Temple of Marttand or the Sun. Niche in the interior.—figure representing the Sun.
Probable date A.D. 490 to 555. No. 14. '68.

KASHMIR.

Temple of MARTTAND OR THE SUN. Niche in the interior.—figure representing the Sun.
Probable date A.D. 490 to 555. No. 15. '68.

KASHMIR.

Temple of MARTTAND OR THE SUN. Niche in the interior—female figure, probable representing one of the Sun's wives, "the Moon in conjunction," "Intellect," or "Brightness."
Probable date A.D. 390 to 555. No. 16. '68.

KASHMIR.

KASHMIR.

Temple of Marttand or the Sun. View of Peristyle, North side of Enclosure. Probable date A.D. 693 to 729. No. 19. '68.

TEMPLE AT BHANIYAR.*

THIS Temple is of great interest, as it shows at a glance what form all those of Kashmir took. It is the most perfect in the valley, and could only have escaped destruction by the Mahomedans on account of its remote situation.

Bhaniyar is on the left bank of the Jhelum, about 1¾ miles beyond Naoshera, and is on the road leading out of Kashmir towards Murree. At present the temple is occupied by an old Hindu Fakeer, who asserts that the erection of the building dates some thousands of years ago, and was the work of the Pandus, a race of giants. The style of the central edifice and colonnade, or peristyle, fixes the time of their construction about the sixth or seventh centuries. Some few years ago, this temple was completely embedded in the earth, which had been washed down from the mountains behind it. The Raja of Kashmir had it excavated, and at present, the colonnade is quite perfect.

General Cunningham is of opinion that the name Bhaniyar, or Bhawaniyar, implies that the temple was dedicated to the goddess Bhawani, the wife of Siva.

---

* See Photographs 37 and 38—'68.

KASHMIR.

Temple at Bhaniyar on the road between Uri and Naoshera. The Temple probably dedicated to the goddess "Bhawani," the wife of "Siva." Probable date A.D. 500 to 600 (?) No. 37. '68.

KASHMIR.

Part of the Colonnade of Temple at Bhaniyar on the road between Uri and Naoshera. The Temple probably dedicated to the goddess "Bhawani," the wife of "Siva."

Probable date A.D. 500 to 600 (?)

No. 38.'68.

RUINS AT AVANTIPORE.

THE present village of Avantipore is about 18 miles from Srinagar, and on the right bank of the Jhelum. Although now but a mere hamlet of a few peasants' houses, it was, when first built by Avanti Varmma, between A.D. 852 and 883, a place of considerable importance. Scarcely anything remains except the foundations and outlines of the colonnades of two temples, the erection of which, is ascribed by the Rajah Tarangini, also to Avanti Varmma. "This wise one," he says, "erected Avantiswámi before he became king, and Avanteswara after "he had attained sovereignty." Both these temples of Avantiswami and Avanteswara, were dedicated to Siva, as implied by their names; and I cannot but think, with General Cunningham, that the smaller temple of Avantiswami was built before Avanti Varmma ascended the throne, and the larger one of Avanteswara, when a kingly wealth put the means into his hands of indulging in more ambitious dimensions. It might, however, be argued that no evidence exists of the amount of elaboration expended on the larger temple; whilst on the other hand, we know that the smaller one of Avantiswami was not only covered throughout with sculptures, but surrounded also by a handsome colonnade, in which great variety and beauty of ornamental detail was displayed.

The Brahmans are of the same opinion as General Cunningham, so that there is sufficient reason for holding that the name of the larger temple was Avanteswara, and that of the smaller Avantiswami. Avanti Varmma ascended the throne in A.D. 854; the erection, therefore, of Avantiswami may be conjectured as occurring about 852–854.

Photograph No. 20—'68 gives a general view of the ruins, and a reference to drawing No. 3—'68 will explain the disposition of the various parts of the central temple and colonnade as they now exist. The amount of elaboration in the decoration, must have been great, as in addition to those parts of the colonnade which have been excavated,* and which enabled a restoration to be made of the peristyle,† a great quantity of carved stonework is strewn all over the pile of ruins, which now occupy the site of the central temple.

The Gateway, as photographed in Nos. 21, 23, and 24, gives some idea of the enormous extent to which the surface decoration was carried.

The Temple of Avanteswara‡ is completely ruined, and with the exception of a small portion of the colonnade and the gateway,§ scarcely anything remains to mark the form of the buildings. The date of erection may be assumed to be between A.D. 854-888, the period of Avanti Varmma's reign; and if the height of the temple followed the same proportion of the breadth, which is common in all other temples, it must have been the loftiest building in India. The width is 85 feet; the height would therefore have been 170 feet.

---

* See Photograph No. 22—'68.

† See Drawing No. 2—'68.

‡ See Drawing 4—'68; Photograph 25—'68.

§ See Photographs 26 and 27—'68.

KASHMIR.

General View of Ruins of Temple of Avantiswami at Avantipore. Probable date A.D. 852 to 854.

No. 20. '68

KASHMIR.

Temple of AVANTISWAMI at AVANTIPORE. Gateway of Colonnade from the North East.
Probable date A.D. 852 to 854. No. 21. '68.

KASHMIR.

Temple of Avantiswami at Avantipore. Excavated North East corner of Colonnade.
Probable date A.D. 852 to 854. No. 22. '68.

KASHMIR.

Temple of Avantiswami at Avantipore. Gateway of Colonnade from South East.
Probable date A.D. 852 to 854. No. 23. '68.

KASHMIR.

Temple of AVANTISWAMI at AVANTIPORE. Gateway of Colonnade from South West.
Probable date A.D. 852 to 854. No. 24. '68.

KASHMIR

RESTORATION.

2.-'68.

PERISTYLE of TEMPLE of AVANTISWAMI AT AVANTIPORE.

PROBABLE DATE-A.D. 852-854.

ELEVATION.

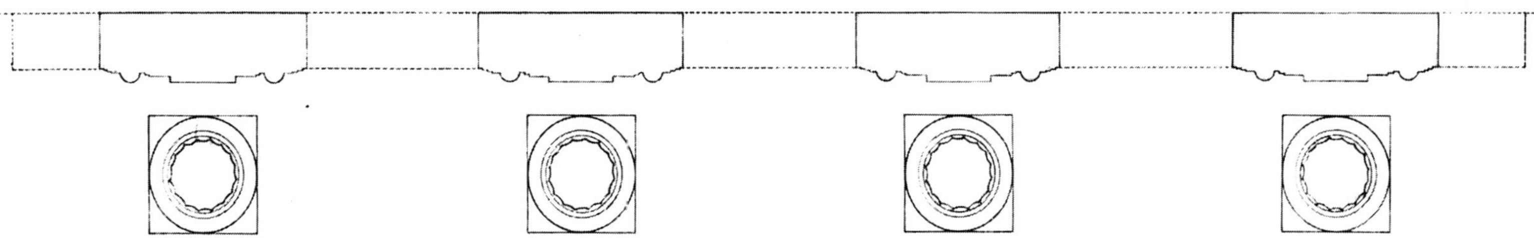

PLAN.

SCALE of FEET

J. F. Rippon

W. GRIGGS. DEL. & LITH.

H. H. Cole
Lieut. R.E.
Supt. Arch. Survey of India
North Western Provinces

INDIA MUSEUM, LONDON 1869.

KASHMIR.

RESTORATION.

3.-'68.

COLONNADE AND TEMPLE OF AVANTISWAMI AT AVANTIPORE.

PROBABLE DATE A.D. 852-854.

EAST

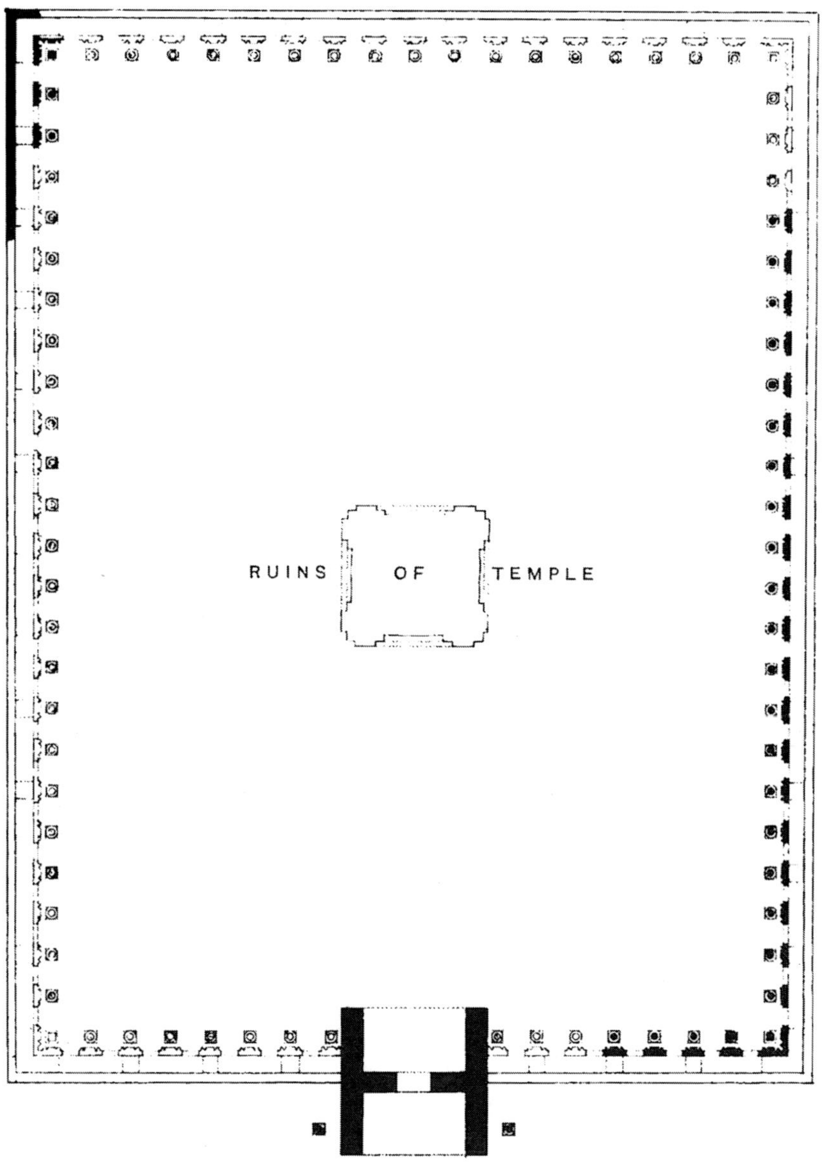

WEST

REFERENCE

EXISTING / RESTORED — PORTIONS

GENERAL PLAN.

SCALE OF FEET

W. GRIGGS. DEL. & LITH.

INDIA MUSEUM, LONDON 1869.

KASHMIR

RESTORATION.

12.-'68.

DETAILS OF SMALL PILLARS AND CAPITALS IN THE COLONNADE OF THE TEMPLE OF AVANTISWAMI AT AVANTIPORE.

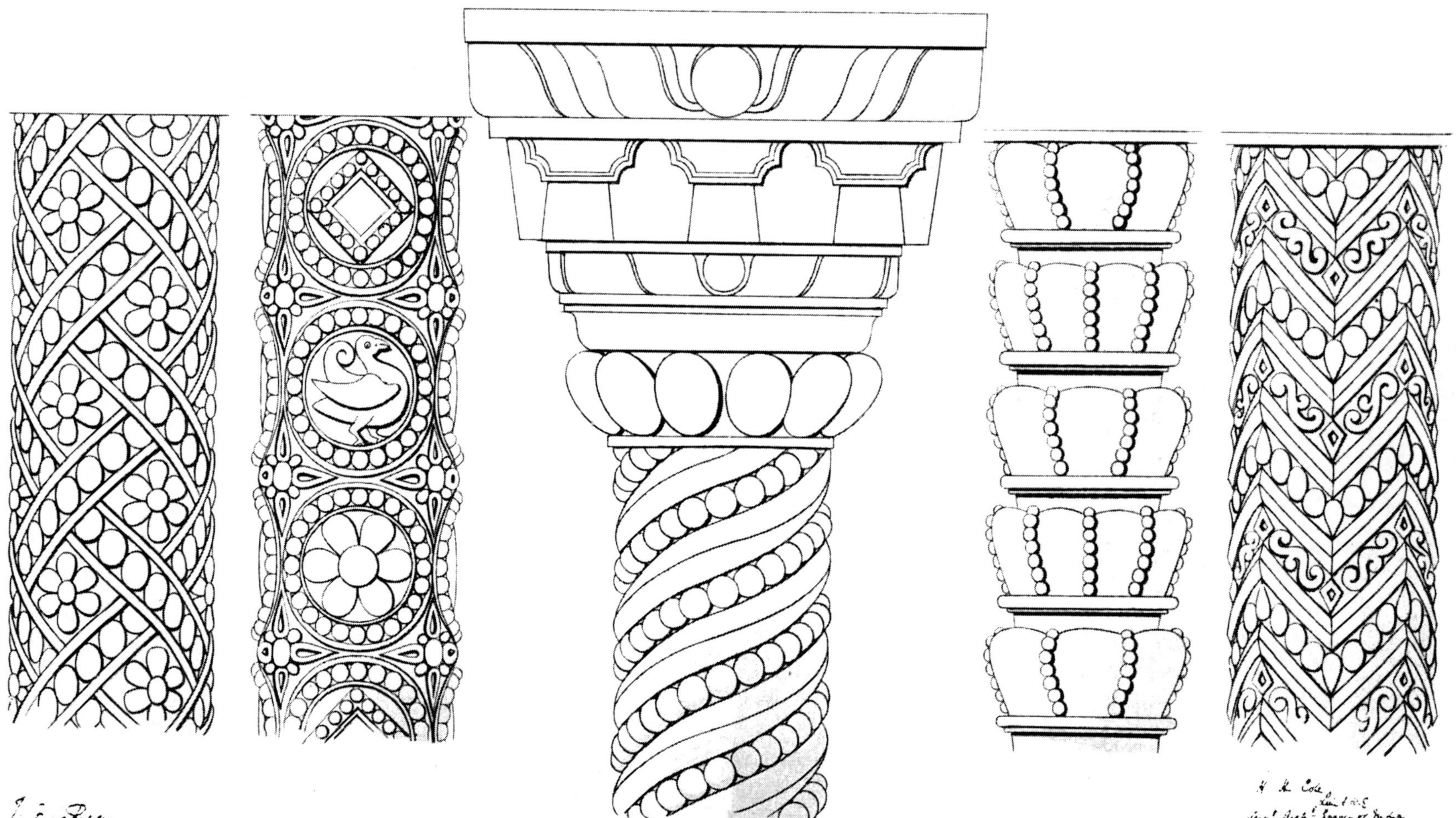

W. GRIGGS. DEL. & LITH.

INDIA MUSEUM, LONDON 1869.

KASHMIR.

RESTORATION.

12A.-'68.

SKETCH OF A DRUM OF ONE OF THE SMALL PILLARS IN THE COLONNADE OF THE TEMPLE OF AVANTISWAMI AT AVANTIPORE.

W. GRIGGS. DEL. & LITH.

INDIA MUSEUM, LONDON 1869.

KASHMIR.

General View of Temple of AVANTESWARA near AVANTIPORE. Probable date A.D. 854 to 888.
No. 25. '68.

KASHMIR.

Temple of AVANTESWARA near AVANTIPORE. View of Gateway of enclosure from West.
Probable date A.D. 854 to 888. No. 26. '68.

KASHMIR.

Temple of AVANTESWARA near AVANTIPORE. View of Gateway of Enclosure from North West.
Probable date A.D. 854 to 888. No. 27. '68.

KASHMIR. 4.-'68.

RESTORATION.

COLONNADE AND TEMPLE OF AVANTESWARA
NEAR AVANTIPORE.
PROBABLE DATE A.D. 854-888.

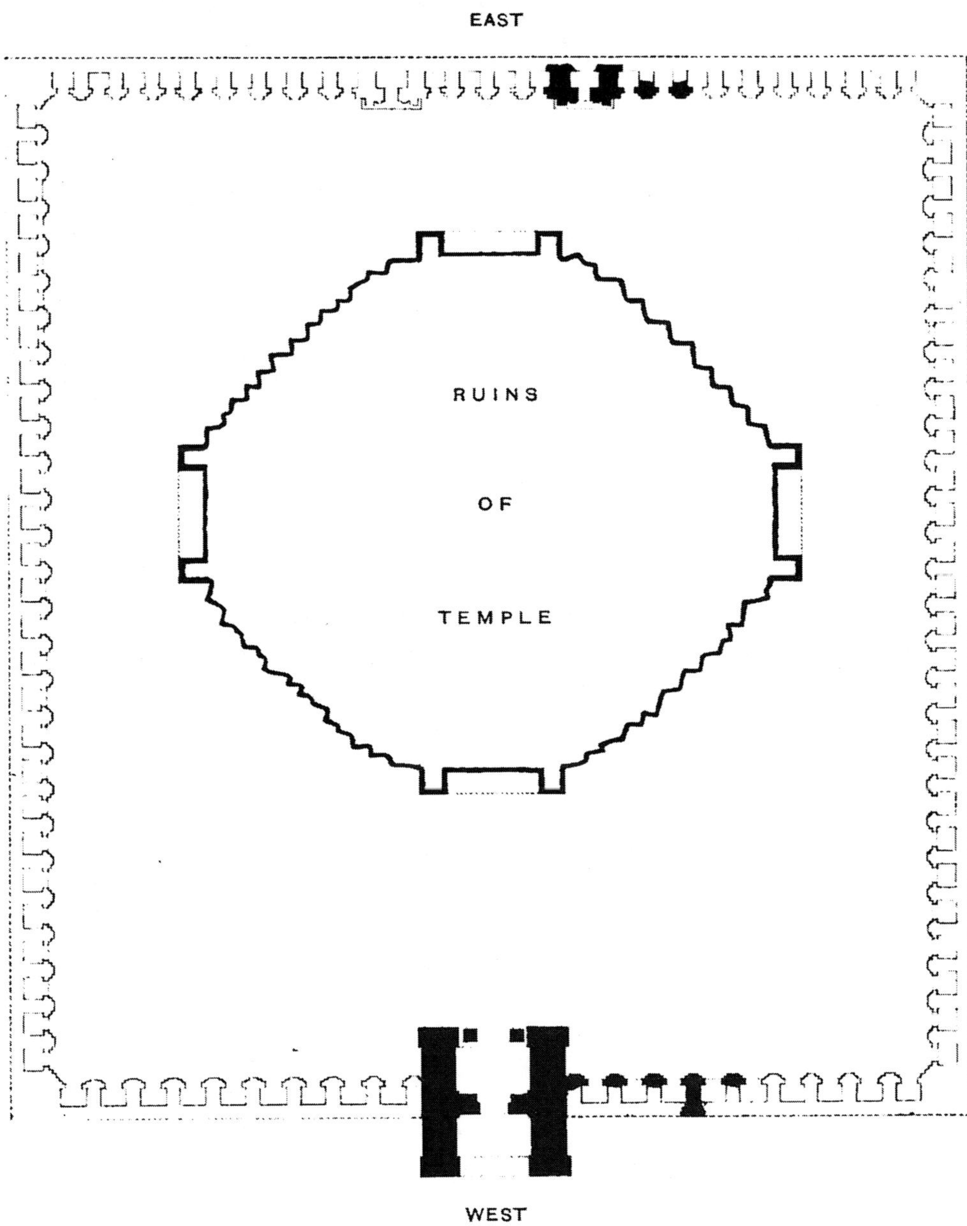

REFERENCE

Existing } Portions
Restored }

GENERAL PLAN.

SCALE OF FEET.

H. H. Cole, Lieut R.E.
Supt. Archl. Survey of India
North Western Provinces.

W. GRIGGS. DEL. & LITH.

INDIA MUSEUM, LONDON 1869.

TEMPLES AT PATHAN.

PATHAN is situated on the high road between Srinagar and Baramula, and is about sixteen miles from the capital.

It is supposed that a king named Sankara Varmma, who reigned between 883 and 901, erected the two temples near this village.* The two Buildings are rather less than half a mile apart, and the Raja Tarangini records them thus: " This prince (Sankara Varmma), equal to the King of Gods (Indra), in con- " junction with her (his wife Sugandha), erected in that excellent town (San- " kara-pura or Pathan) temples to Sankara gauresa and to Sughandeósá."

As General Cunningham says, it would appear probable that the larger Temple was built by the King, and the lesser one built in the name of the Queen.

The plan of the Temple of Sugandheswara is like those of the buildings at Avantipore; the roof was pyramidal, and must have been about 48 feet high. A quadrangle probably existed, as the ruins of a gateway and of a wall, are still traceable at a distance of about 60 feet from the eastern face.

The Temple of Sankara Gaureswara is elaborately carved, and some of the details are as sharp and clear as when first cut. The degree of elaboration in the porch-like projections and interior carvings, tend to confirm the traditional writings of the Raja Tarangini, in respect of the date of foundation.

The repetition of the pediments one above the other, together with the highly decorated pillars in the porches, all prove that the style of building practised in Kashmir since the erection of the Jyeshteswara Temple, had in the progress of time followed the natural tendency for greater elaboration.

---

* See Photographs 28, 29, 30, 31, 33, 34, 35—'68.

KASHMIR.

Temple of SANKARAGAURESWARA near the Village of PATHAN. View of North face.
Probable date A.D. 883 to 901. No. 28. '68.

KASHMIR.

Temple of SANKARAGAURESWARA near the Village of PATHAN. View of West Face.
Probable date A.D. 883 to 901. No. 29. '68.

KASHMIR.

Temple of SANKARAGAURESWARA near the Village of PATHAN. View from South East.
Probable date A.D. 883 to 901. No. 30. '68.

KASHMIR.

Temple of SANKARAGAURESWARA near the Village of PATHAN. Niche on the left of Entrance.
Probable date A.D. 883 to 901. No. 31. '68.

KASHMIR.

Ruins of a Temple at NORWAH. The Temple is circular in the interior and square externally, it is about 14 feet underground and should be excavated. Only the North Face is standing. No. 32. '68.

KASHMIR.

Temple of SUGANDHESWARA near Village of PATHAN. View of South Face.
Probable date A.D. 883 to 901. No. 33. '68.

KASHMIR.

Temple of SUGANDHESWARA near Village of PATHAN. View of South Face.
Probable date A.D. 883 to 901. No. 34. '68.

KASHMIR.

Temple of SUGANDHESWARA near Village of PATHAN. View of East Face.
Probable date A.D. 883 to 901. No. 35. '68.

KASHMIR.

View of a Bhuddhist Tope near Baramula. The locality which includes the remains of a Monastery is called the "Jayendra Vihar," and the erection is assigned by local tradition to one "Praverasena" in A.D. 500.
Excavation required. No. 36. '68.

TEMPLE AT PANDRETHAN.

THE small village of Pandrethan is situated on the Jhelum, about a mile and a half to the south-east of Srinagar. The name Pandrethan is derived from "Puranadhisthana," which means the "Old Capital," and there is no doubt but that an ancient city existed at this place, which to the present day is strewn with remains. The Temple is close to the village, and stands in the centre of a tank of water. The Raja Tarangini says that a minister named Meru, erected a Temple called Sri-Meru-Varddhana-swami at Pandrethan, and that the building occurred between the years A.D. 913 and 921, and as this is the only Temple recorded as having existed at Pandrethan, there is every reason to suppose that the existing Temple and that of Sri-Meru-Varddhana-swami are one and the same.*

At the time of my visit, the water was about two feet over the floor of the Temple, and I had to obtain a small boat to enable me and my surveyors to take measurements, &c.

The stone ceiling is elaborately carved in bas-relief figures, and is one of the most perfect pieces of ancient carving that exists in Kashmir.

In this building, the later date of erection established by history, becomes also apparent in the greater degree of elaboration in the general style. The pyramidal roof is divided into two portions by an ornamental band. The corner pilasters are surmounted by carved capitals,† and the pediments of the porches appear to have terminated with a melon-shaped ornament. The ceiling is formed of nine blocks of stone; four resting over the angles of the cornice, reduce the opening to a square, and an upper course of four

---

* See Drawing 9—'68, and Photographs 40, 41, 42—'68.

† See Drawing 11—'68.

stones still further reduces the opening, which is covered by a single block decorated with a large lotus.*

The square form of the tank surrounding the building, would indicate an enclosure of some kind, but there exist no traces of pillars or trefoil-headed arches.

---

* See Drawing No. 10—'68.

KASHMIR.

Temple of Meruvarddhanaswami at Pandrethan near Srinagar. View of South West Face.
Probable date A.D. 913 to 921. No. 40. '68.

KASHMIR.

Temple of Meruvarddhanaswami at Pandrethan near Srinagar. View of North Face.

Probable date A.D. 913 to 921. No. 41. '68.

KASHMIR.

Temple of MERUVARDDHANASWAMI at PANDRETHAN near SRINAGAR. Probable date A.D. 913 to 921.

View of North West Face. No. 42. '68.

KASHMIR.

RESTORATION.

9.-'68.

TEMPLE OF MERUVARDDHANASWAMI, AT PANDRETHAN NEAR SRINAGAR,

PROBABLE DATE-A.D. 913-921.

ELEVATION

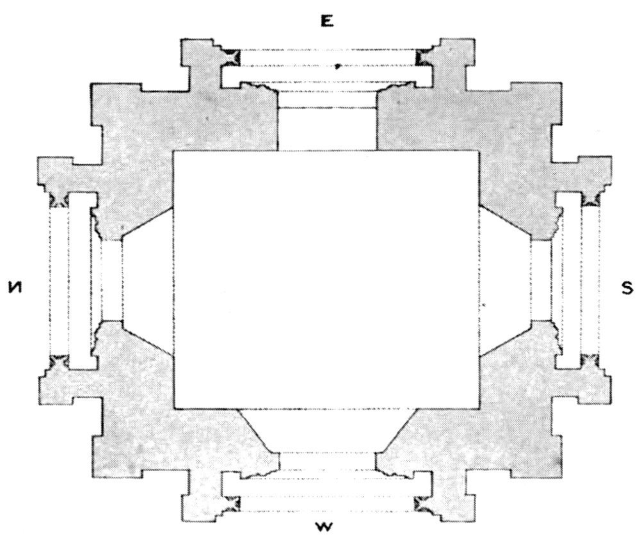

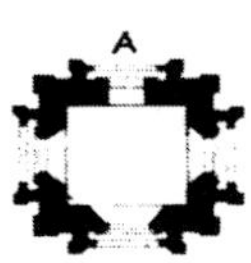

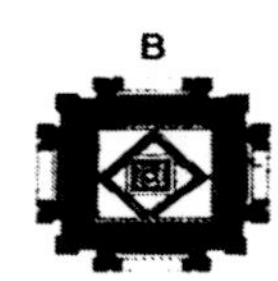

PLAN

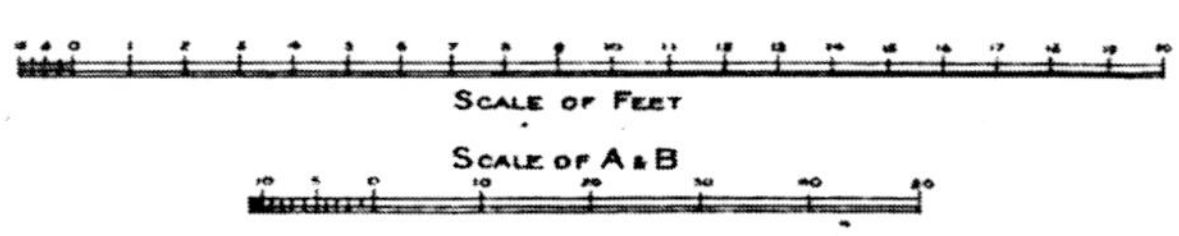

W. GRIGGS. DEL. & LITH.

H. H. Cole Lieut. R.E.
Supt. Archl. Survey of India
North Western Provinces

INDIA MUSEUM, LONDON 1869.

KASHMIR.

RESTORATION.

10.–'68.

TEMPLE AT PANDRETHAN, NEAR SRINAGAR.

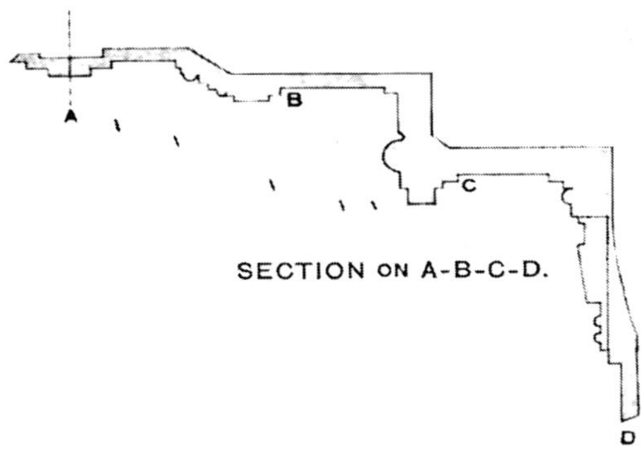

SECTION ON A-B-C-D.

PLAN OF CEILING.

W. GRIGGS. DEL. & LITH.

H. H. Cole
Lieut. R.E.
Supt. Arch. Survey of India
North Western Provinces

INDIA MUSEUM, LONDON 1869.

SCALE OF FEET

KASHMIR.

RESTORATION.

11.-'68.

FRAGMENT OF STONE SCULPTURE,
FOUND NEAR THE TEMPLE
AT PANDRETHAN.

THE CAPITAL PROBABLY OF A PILASTER.

W. GRIGGS. DEL. & LITH.

H. H. Cole, Lieut. R.E.
Supt. Arch. Survey of India
North Western Provinces.

INDIA MUSEUM, LONDON 1869.

PILLAR NEAR THE JUMMA MUSJID IN SRINAGAR.

PHOTOGRAPH No. 44—'68, is of a beautiful little column on the outside of the Jumma Musjid. The top is crowned by a perfect little Temple, with a roof of three stories, which illustrates the style of sacred edifices in Kashmir.

VITCHER NAG.

AT some little distance from Srinagar, and on the road to Gauderbal, there is a Mahomedan Zearut or Burial Ground, which has been built of parts of ruined Hindu Temples. The most perfect portion of the buildings is shown in Photograph 43—'68.

FINIS.

KASHMIR.

Ruins of an old Hindu Temple at Vitcher Nag near Srinagar. Now used as a Mahomedan burial ground.

No. 43. '68.

KASHMIR.

Small Isolated Pillar near the Jumma Musjid (or Big Mosque) in Srinagar. The little Temple on its summit illustrates the style of Kashmirian Edifices. No. 44. '68.